To my own mother tree, who taught me to raise
my own little sap. To my husband, with whom I
share the canopy. And to all the scientists whose
work makes the world a better place.

−JH

For Evi,
do what you love, keep growing.

−RH

Book design by Melissa Nelson Greenberg

Library of Congress Cataloging-in-Publication Data available.
ISBN: 978-1-951836-06-1

Printed in China

10 9 8 7 6 5 4 3

CAMERON KIDS is an imprint of CAMERON + COMPANY

CAMERON + COMPANY
Petaluma, California
www.cameronbooks.com

Little Sap

The magical story of a forest family

written by Jan Hughes

illustrated by Ruth Hengeveld

cameron kids

Little Sap lives with her family deep in the heart of a very old forest. She grows near Mother Tree, the tallest and wisest tree in the grove.

Little Sap can't wait to be a mother tree!

In spring, when bluebells carpet the woodlands, Little Sap shows off her newly budding leaves, glistening like jewels in the sunlight.

In summer, the tall trees around her fill the sky with green.

Little Sap reaches as high as she can . . .
but she is still swallowed up by the shade.

Will she ever reach the light?

After the rains, Little Sap's friends the Penny Buns poke their heads through the damp forest floor to say hello.

They bring sweet, soothing treats
from Mother Tree to Little Sap.

Little Sap wants to touch the sky . . .

40 years old

60 years old

80 years old

400 years old

but tree time is very S L O W.

Mother Tree insists that Little Sap doesn't reach
too far, too fast and guides her gently upward.

Grow slow, little one . . . take your time . . .
Stand up straight . . . turn this way . . .
You'll get there one day . . .
The slower you grow, the stronger you'll be.

High summer is a busy time in the forest.

Birds make their way to their favorite branches . . .
Squirrels run up and down and all around . . .
Insects chirp in a rousing chorus . . .

. . . and pesky bugs come to feast on the trees!

When Little Sap feels the bugs munching on her beautiful leaves, Mother Tree warns the family and sends a fragrant cloud to scare off the pests.

In fall, the forest quiets down and becomes cloaked in amber.

The trees shed their leaves and store food and water,
preparing for a long winter's slumber.

Little Sap clings to her leaves as long as she can, gobbling
up a bit more sunlight before the season ends.

In winter, as the days get shorter and snow flurries dance around her, Little Sap finally settles down to sleep.

Every spring, Little Sap gets closer to the light . . .
one day taking her place in the sun-filled canopy.

A mother tree—
with a little sap of her own.

FOREST FAMILIES

When you walk through a forest, what do you see? Beautiful, majestic, quiet trees. But are they really quiet? Trees are actually very talkative—you just can't hear them. To understand trees, you have to look beneath the soil. Aboveground, trees share their quiet beauty with the world and use their leaves to make food. Belowground, they are very busy chatting, sharing, and caring.

MOTHER TREES

The largest trees in the forest, known as mother trees, feed the young and take care of hundreds of other trees. How do they do this? With the help of their friends, the fungi!

When you see mushrooms in the forest, just like apples on a tree, they are the fruit of the fungal colonies whose long, fine threads spread throughout the soil. These underground colonies, which can be thousands of years old, connect the roots of the trees with one another and enable the mother trees to share food and information.

Mother trees share a fair amount of their food with the fungi, who cannot make their own. In exchange, the fungi deliver food, water, nutrients, and important messages to the forest. Baby trees, or saplings, who don't get enough sunlight to make their own food, are fed this way. A German forester, Peter Wohlleben, discovered that an elderly tree who was nothing more than an ancient stump (after having been chopped down hundreds of years before) was being kept alive with the help of her forest family. Perhaps she was a once-revered mother tree! Professor of forest ecology Suzanne Simard, who studies how trees communicate with one another, discovered that mother trees send electrical signals through their roots to guide saplings toward the light as they grow in the darkness of the understory. When old mother trees are dying, after hundreds of years of helping hundreds of trees, they pass their wisdom down to the next generation. The trees and the fungi work together to keep the whole forest family strong and healthy.

SAPLINGS

Young trees, or saplings, grow until they reach the canopy, the leafy tippy-top of the forest, where they can drink in the sunlight and make food with their leaves. But tree time is very slow—in some forests, it can take hundreds of years for a sapling to finally reach the sky, as they have to wait for a space to open up in the canopy, which only happens when another tree dies. On their journey toward the light, mother trees insist that the young take their time—the more slowly they grow, the stronger they will be. You can tell how old a tree is by looking at the rings in their trunk; each ring represents a year. Some species of trees can live for five thousand years!

WONDROUS TREES

Not only do they have families, trade goods, and take care of each other, but some scientists think that in their own way trees can also taste, smell, see, hear, and count. Trees can taste the saliva of certain harmful bugs and then release a scent cloud to warn other trees and attract helpful insects to come to their rescue. Trees can see, following the light as they grow. Trees can hear, detecting signals sent by other trees. Trees can even count the warm days in spring so they know when to open their buds. Amazing!

Trees are our oldest companions, having been on earth for hundreds of millions of years! Trees help us breathe, cleaning the air and giving us oxygen. They keep us cool and give us paper, wood, and fruit. What can we give trees in return? The chance for them and their forest families to remain healthy and strong. Let's protect mother trees and leave the forests to do what they have been doing for millions of years.

FOREST WHISPERERS

The story of Little Sap and her fictional forest family was inspired by the work of biologists, ecologists, foresters, and naturalists who have been sharing their research with the world. For more on the wonders and language of nature, look up the work of Suzanne Simard, Peter Wohlleben, Monica Gagliano, and David George Haskell, among others.